# WALKING IN
# Watercolor

## An Artist's Pilgrimage on the Camino de Santiago

Jennifer Lawson

with Patricia Lennon

For information, please contact: info@jlawsonart.com

Printed in the United States of America

First Printing, 2017

ISBN-13: 978-0692860618

Jennifer Lawson
PO Box 2908
South Portland, ME 04116
www.jlawsonart.com

## Acknowledgments

We wish to thank our families and dear friends who encouraged us at every step. We are especially grateful for our rich community of friends and colleagues who freely shared their creative expertise, advice, and knowledge. Finally, to our fellow pilgrims who inspired us along The Way.

Book Design: Visible Logic, Inc.
This creative team brought just the right combination of structure and finesse to a project that challenged us all.

Editor: MorningStar Editing, LLC
To Cassie Armstrong who enjoyed taking the walk with us through our words, genuinely supported the project, and made sure all the references to Spain were spelled correctly.

Manuscript Evaluation: Tom Sidar
Who made absolutely sure that my voice stayed true to who I am.

2 Friends
32 Days
500 Miles
1 Amazing Journey

Santiago
de Compostela

Sarria

Cruz de Ferro

Leon

Sahagun

Camino

ATLANTIC OCEAN

PORTUGAL

FRANCE

St Jean Pied de Port

Roncesvalles

Pamplona

Logrono

Castrojeriz

Burgos

de Santiago

SPAIN

Buen Camino

# In the spring of 2014, we went on a really long walk...

My longtime friend Patti and I decided to walk the Camino de Santiago for an important birthday milestone. We read about it, trained for it, and I decided to put my art to the test. I would sketch every day—watercolors over ink—quick and loose, to capture gesture, form, light, and color—and I hope on this journey—meaning.

A pilgrimage is seeking in its purest form. It is a progression toward something more. For each of us, it is our own personal journey. So, with packs on our backs that for five weeks would be our dressers, closets, medicine cabinet, pantries, and for me my art studio, we would walk 500 miles following scallop shells and yellow arrows to Santiago de Compostela.

I am an artist. I am a hiker. And now I was in a line of pilgrims waiting to get our required passports to walk the Camino. These passports would be stamped daily at *albergues* (pilgrim only hostels), cafés, bars, and churches during the route to Santiago and serve as proof of our pilgrimage, where we would receive an official Pilgrims Certificate, or *compostela*, for completing the walk.

Our journey started on a cool misty spring day in St Jean Pied de Port, France, at the base of the Pyrenees Mountains.

# Day 1
## St Jean Pied de Port, France to Roncesvalles, Spain
25.1 km/15.6 miles

Day 1 was a steep 15-mile hike. Shouldering our packs for the first time, we climbed up and over the high mountain pass of the Pyrenees. With scallop shells hanging on our packs identifying us as pilgrims, we set off for Roncesvalles, Spain. A ninety percent chance of rain and thunderstorms kept us moving. While passing small hillside farms and open pastures, a very friendly mountain dog started walking with us—we named him "Jean Luc". He would lead the way for a while and then wait for us to catch up. If we stopped for water or to rest, he sat dutifully next to us.

We arrived in Roncesvalles cold, wet, and tired. I hugged Jean Luc and bid him *au revoir* and we headed off to check in for our first night after a long day on the Camino.

The next morning Jean Luc was gone.

# Day 2  Roncesvalles to Zubiri
22 km/13.7 miles

It was drizzling and quite cold as we set out on Day 2 of our pilgrimage. Dressed in our rain gear, we started to walk, pulling our sleeves over our hands to fend off the chill. As we left Roncesvalles, we passed the famous sign that shows 790 kilometers to Santiago. We followed the yellow arrows through beautiful wooded forests, alongside wide green pastures dotted with sheep, and quaint villages with whitewashed red-roofed cottages. Perfect places to stop, rest, and sketch, but weather and the unknown kept us moving.

EL PALO DE AVELLANO
albergue zubin

Continuing our steep descent, we cut across grassy pastures where I had to avoid stepping on the extremely large black slugs on the path. Patti explained their importance to the forest's ecosystem, but I still say, "YUCK—European Black Slugs!"

The skies began to clear as we crossed a medieval stone bridge over the Río Arga to enter the town of Zubiri, Spain. We found our *albergue*, then enjoyed the late afternoon sitting in the sun while visiting with pilgrims Andy and Jaki, who we met when traveling from the United States to Spain. I sketched and we shared stories until it was time to search for food at the local *mercado*, or grocery store. Hungry, I wondered how many calories I had burned in the past two days...

ZUBIRI

# Day 3 Zubiri to Cizur Menor
## 26 km/16.2 miles

The walled city of Pamplona where the Camino runs right through its historic heart.

After walking almost 15 miles, we were inside the ancient walls of the famous city of Pamplona. The crowded streets were lively and festive. My shoulders were burning from the weight of my pack and I suddenly felt sick and needed to sit. We found a park in a quieter part of the city and stopped at a bench so I could remove my pack and give my shoulders a break. I immediately felt better and began to rummage in my pack for something to eat. After finding some of those delicious European digestive cookies, I ate the entire package before we set off to find our *albergue* in the village of Cizur Menor just beyond Pamplona.

The next day we continued through the rolling hills of the Navarre region of Spain. The colorful landscape is a patchwork of crops dominated by fields of bright yellow flowers, which is rapeseed, grown for making canola oil.

Vibrant yellow flowers of rapeseed are grown to produce canola oil.

# Day 4 Cizur Menor to Puente la Reina
## 19 km/11.8 miles

Every day pilgrims leave the village of St Jean Pied de Port, France, and begin their journey to Santiago de Compostela, Spain. Some of the pilgrims who started their walk the same day as we did became welcome faces along the way. We shared the same path, the same weather, the same pain, and the same joy. One of the great pleasures of the Camino is the spontaneous friendships that happen when walking—like old friends, we would fall into step, exchange stories, stop for a break at a roadside café, or share a bunk in a room at an *albergue*. There is clearly a strong sense of belonging on the Camino.

# Day 5 Puente la Reina to Estella
## 21.9 km/13.6 miles

Crossing the pilgrim's bridge out of Puente la Reina, Patti stopped and said she wasn't able to walk to the next destination. She was feeling extreme pain in her Achilles tendon from her stiff leather hiking boots. She thought a day of rest would be the best solution and said she would meet me in Estella via taxi.

*Crunch, click, crunch, click, crunch* was the only sound I heard when my boots and hiking poles touched the ground as I made my way toward Estella. I wandered along the red earth road, passing through vineyards and olive groves of the Navarre region. As I crossed over the Río Arga on the ancient pilgrim's bridge, I worried about Patti and the fate of our journey to Santiago...

Patti and I made it to Estella in different ways. Estella is a big enough town for a sporting goods store, so for a whopping 200 euros she had a pair of trail running shoes that would take her to Santiago.

An old stone bridge on a stretch of ancient Roman road.

## Journaling

A pilgrim's life is being a wanderer in another land… being open to the people and places you come across on the journey. The end of a day is a time for sharing with other pilgrims and for personal reflection. Most pilgrims found joy in writing in a journal, but for me, it was an ink pen, a brush, watercolors, and my sketchbook that captured my memories.

ALBERGUE JUVENIL MUNICIPAL
ONCINEDA
ESTELLA LIZARRA

# Day 6

## Estella to Los Arcos
21.1 km/13.1 miles

**W**ith a new pair of shoes, Patti was back on the Camino. Our days started with Patti dutifully stretching her Achilles tendon while I searched for a *café con leche* and maybe a quick sketch, or better yet—both!

About an hour after leaving Estella, we came upon la Fuente del Vino de Bodegas Irache or Fuente de Irache—the infamous wine fountain. Apparently, pilgrims consume thousands of liters of ***"free wine"*** each year from this fountain that suddenly appears in a grassy field in the middle of nowhere. It was very early in the morning when we stared at this unusual phenomenon—***"free wine"***.

**BODEGAS IRÁCHE**
DESDE 1891

A fellow pilgrim asked if we would take his picture drinking from the fountain. We agreed but first I had to show him how to set up for the photo. "Like this," I said as Patti snapped my photo. Laughing and appreciative of my creative art direction, he got into "wine drinking" position and we took his picture. We wished each other a *¡Buen Camino!* and he happily wandered off with several water bottles filled with ***"free wine"!***

# Day 7  Los Arcos to Logroño
## 28.6 km/17.8 miles

We have now walked 100 miles and are one-fifth of the way to Santiago. When we stopped to take a break for water and food, I was thankful to be able to take my pack off and give my shoulders a much-needed break. Too tired to eat, I rested my head on my pack, knowing that I would be carrying it again soon for the last 5 miles into Logroño, Spain.

In addition to my sore collarbones, I felt the slight burn of a blister on my baby toe. Patti had her own set of aches and pains. Thankfully, the European extra-strength Ibuprofen helped. Every morning we prepped our feet with anti-blister balm and bandages, if needed. We capped sore toes with an amazing find, mineral oil infused gel toe caps, that protected our toes from further injury and pain.

After wending our way through the city and settling into our *albergue*, we sat at an outdoor café on the Plaza Mercado. While enjoying a *vino blanco*, I did a quick sketch before we went in search of some famous Logroño tapas. When we arrived at the street filled with tapas bars, it was cordoned off and a police officer was keeping people out. Curious, we asked what the problem was, and he said an "oil spill". "Olive oil?" I shouted over the crowd. He flashed a smile and pointed to a detour. We then indulged in the most artfully beautiful and delicious tapas imaginable.

HOSTEL
ENTRESUEÑOS
Telf. 941 271334
LOGROÑO

KARMA

Plaza Mercado, Longrono, Spain

olives

pimentos

jamon

salmon

spinach

artichoke

jamon

asparagas

omelette

cerezas

aceituna

zanahorias

digestive cookies

DIGESTIVE

DIGE

tortitas de mais con jamon

# Walk, Eat, Sleep

Carrying a pack, dressing to deal with changing weather conditions, taking care of your feet, and finding a place to sleep at the end of the day are all part of a pilgrim's daily routine. However, there comes a time on the walk when you realize you are amazingly hungry and the need for food supersedes everything else. Our eating habits became somewhat out of character as the miles and days wore on...and on...and on...

We came to love the hearty, satisfying food of Spain that we enjoyed at local cafés, pilgrim's dinners, and carried in our packs. Our favorite memories—a glass of local *vino blanco*, or a cerveza, a bowl of delicious Spanish olives, sitting with a table full of pilgrims, and me with my sketch book.

cervesa

bocadillo de jamon

vino Blanco

huevos duras

tortilla de patatas

23

# Day 8

## Logroño to Ventosa
19.7 km/12.2 miles

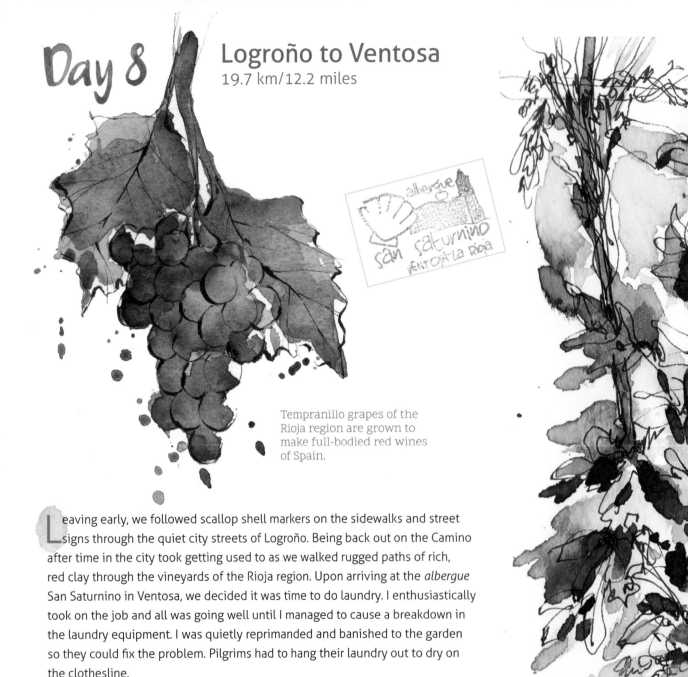

Tempranillo grapes of the Rioja region are grown to make full-bodied red wines of Spain.

Leaving early, we followed scallop shell markers on the sidewalks and street signs through the quiet city streets of Logroño. Being back out on the Camino after time in the city took getting used to as we walked rugged paths of rich, red clay through the vineyards of the Rioja region. Upon arriving at the *albergue* San Saturnino in Ventosa, we decided it was time to do laundry. I enthusiastically took on the job and all was going well until I managed to cause a breakdown in the laundry equipment. I was quietly reprimanded and banished to the garden so they could fix the problem. Pilgrims had to hang their laundry out to dry on the clothesline.

While I hung my head, I found a place in the sun and sketched the drying laundry as I worried about that nagging blister on my baby toe. Where is that ***"free wine"*** fountain when you need it?

Albergue San Saturnino
Ventosa, Spain

albergue
san saturnino
Ruta la Rioja
Tel:

# Day 9 Ventosa to Santo Domingo
31.4 km/19.5 miles

Tired and cold, we wandered through the ancient medieval town of Santo Domingo de la Calzada, best known for having a chicken coop in the cathedral. We then found the *albergue* run by Cistercian nuns, paid a donation fee, and checked in. We were led up creaky old stairs, down a hallway with a definite slant, into a very small cramped room with four beds, which were all very close to each other, and an inhumanly loud snoring sound coming from a room very nearby... "It's a 'snoring machine,'" I whispered to Patti.

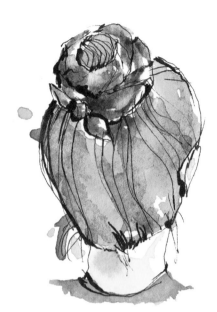

End of day
evening scrunchie

Bandana

Fake hair
scrunchie

Walking was easy in comparison to the daily routine of packing and repacking, organizing, showering and drying off with a tiny travel towel, and sleeping with twelve to twenty-four snoring pilgrims in bunk beds. On top of all of that...was my hair. I wore it up to keep it out of the way and to look as stylish as Camino possible. I brought a handful of hair ornaments, including a fake hairpiece. Every day, I would put my hair up without a mirror and ask Patti how it looked. If she gave me the thumbs up, we were on our way. I wore the fake hairpiece when we were in search of dinner in Santo Domingo de la Calzada. It was quite windy and suddenly the hairpiece flew off my head and started rolling down the busy cobblestone street. I chased it down and stuffed it in my pack...I don't think anyone noticed...

# Day 10 Santo Domingo to Belorado
22.9 km/14.2 miles

The charming Plaza Mayor
is a favorite gathering place
in Belorado.

**W**e arrived in Belorado, a small town of 6,000, where locals and pilgrims were enjoying a warm sunny afternoon at outdoor cafés around the town square. Patti and I consumed our usual after walk snack—*vino blanco*, cerveza, and *papas fritas*—the local white wine for me, Spanish beer for Patti, and the satisfying crunch of a bag of potato chips.

cervesa

vino blanco

papas fritas

We were becoming accustomed to our lives as pilgrims. Most days commenced before the sun came up as people donned headlamps and began to rustle around, getting ready to start their day. About this time, with electric toothbrush in hand, I would get an early jump on the shared washrooms.

We would then check the weather and dress accordingly. Feet were prepped and we began to organize and repack. As usual, my stuff was everywhere—on the bed, under the bed, and scattered around the perimeter, while Patti was neatly organized. It is said that "Everyone's Camino is different"... mine was just a little messier.

# Day 11 Belorado to Agés
27.9 km/17.3 miles

Much of the day's walk was on earthen paths in the open countryside before a long 15km/9.3mi uphill climb. Then we walked through woodlands of oak and pine forest before dropping back down into the town of Agés—population sixty.

We checked into our *albergue* and set out to explore the town's one charming street. We walked up to see the church perched at the top of the hill. With the setting sun and beautiful light, I sketched the church complete with storks, while Patti explored the cluster of old stone buildings.

With only a few places to choose for dinner, we were drawn to the café tables with the bouquets of fresh cut lilacs. We sat outside in the warm evening air and enjoyed our dinner.

# Day 12 Agés to Burgos
22 km/13.7 miles

*Plasa St. Maria Burgos, Spain*

After walking through tranquil pastures and vineyards, the last 10km/6mi walk into Burgos was quite unnerving—it follows along a very busy highway and then circumvents the airport. The path follows a chain link fence through an endless industrial area and busy city streets. We saw pilgrims looking at guidebooks and scratching their heads. Some were actually backtracking. We reread the guide, agreed on a direction, and off we went.

Suddenly, an older man grabbed my backpack. He was speaking loudly in Spanish and shaking his head "NO!" Gesturing us to follow him, he handed us off to his friend who guided us over a bridge to a tranquil walk on the shaded river path. "*Muchas gracias*," we said, and he wished us a *¡Buen Camino!* as we headed off to our hotel near the famous Gothic Cathedral of Santa María, the Catedral de Santa María de Burgos.

I found a quiet place to sketch in the Plaza de Santa María, but I couldn't shake the lack of energy from our daunting walk. After tapas, local wine, and renewed Camino spirit, I sketched this group of Burgos locals contentedly sitting under the budding Plane trees on the lively promenade the Paseo del Espolón.

# Day 13   Burgos to Castrojeriz
41.2 km/25.6 miles

The ruins of a 9th century castle sit high above the town of Castrojeriz.

ALBERGUE
CASA NOSTRA
CASTROJERIZ

Sitting in a small plaza in the quiet town of Castrojeriz, we were so hungry that we ate all the provisions in our packs. Delicious, thinly sliced Jamón *Serrano* (cured Spanish ham) and crunchy corn cakes were a packable snack for me. With my hunger satisfied, I was up for sketching. Several pilgrims watched over my shoulder, engaging in questions about sketching, while we shared our first day of walking Spain's central flat plateau known as the Meseta.

Later at the bar in la Taberna de Antonio, we had the most delicious local sheep cheese cured in olive oil. It was served on homemade bread with more of the dark, rich, buttery olive oil drizzled over the top. Proudly, Antonio served a local red wine. I did a sketch of Antonio, signed it, and gave it to him. I took his picture holding the sketch while his family watched from the kitchen. In return, the food and wine were on the house. Along with the gift of art, we left a big tip.

We crossed a deep valley before climbing a rather steep hill. At the top, we could see our future. Speechless, we gaped...all we could see was the Camino winding on for miles and miles and finally disappearing on the horizon. There were no mountains and no trees. Just field after field of wheat as far as the eye could see. I looked a Patti and said, "Where will we pee?"

We were now in the middle third of the Camino known as the Meseta. It is a part of Spain known for its wide cloudless skies, unbearable heat, and endless flat lands. As we walked, we could hear the elusive cuckoo birds mocking us from the trees with their "cuckoo, cuckoo, cuckoo."

cuckoo
cuckoo
cuckoo
cuckoo
cuckoo
cuckoo
cuckoo
cuckoo

# Day 15 Frómista to Carrión de los Condes
## 20.5 km/12.7 miles

After leaving Frómista, we arrived at the notorious *senda*, or sometimes referred to as "the soulless *senda*"—a white stone gravel path built alongside a busy highway. Our guidebook called it the "pilgrim *autopista*," or the "pilgrim highway," because of the vast numbers of pilgrims following the road here, anxious to push through and get beyond this tiresome long stretch.

We passed our pilgrim friend, Lawrence from Canada, making his way along the path with Wim and Erwin from Holland. These three pilgrims were always a welcome sight, and we would excitedly share Camino adventures over a *café con leche,* cerveza, or local wine while sitting in a plaza along the way. As we slogged our way through the endless Meseta, we didn't see them again for days.

Weary after our long day on the *senda*, we splurged for a night at the Hotel Real Monasterio de San Zoilo, a restored 11th century Romanesque monastery that preserves many of its Renaissance influences.

I gave up drinking Diet Coke years ago, but after a long morning on the Camino, there is nothing like stopping for a Coca-Cola Zero to cure the mid-morning slump. Always over ice with a lemon or a lime, it quenched my thirst and made me deliriously happy.

# Day 16

## Carrión de los Condes
## to Nicolás del Real Camino

32.8 km/20.4 miles

Albergue Laganares

San Nicolás, Spain

**W**alking 20 miles through the endless wheat fields of the Meseta put us in an almost trance-like state, induced by hours of putting one foot in front of the other. The only sounds were of our footsteps and hiking poles and the occasional cry of a cuckoo bird. Sometimes when we walked, we talked. Other times, we were quiet as we made our way to the next stop.

San Nicolás del Real Camino has only one place to stay. The *albergue* owners welcomed us warmly and we settled in. After our long walk, it was nice to sit in the sun and sketch in the warmth of the inviting garden. I then meandered out to the plaza with its tiny church and resident stork.

That night we enjoyed a delicious pilgrim's dinner at the very friendly bar and restaurant before climbing into our bunk beds and falling asleep.

# Beauty along The Way

It was the beginning of spring, and as we walked, flowers unfurled their colorful displays—lilacs, roses, rolling hills of lavender, and fields of bright red poppies. All your senses are heightened on the Camino. You get into the daily rhythm of a pilgrim's life.

We were grateful for the pilgrims we met on the trail and for the wonderful people of Spain, who live in the villages and towns that welcomed us with a hearty meal and a place to sleep.

# Day 17 Nicolás del Real Camino to Calzadilla de los Hermanillos

20.9 km/13 miles

Long shadows fell across the empty street as we left the tiny town of San Nicolás early in the morning. It was a cool morning, but the open treeless Meseta would bring sun and heat to another day of walking on the *senda* and its endless flat horizon. We passed a pilgrim driving his horse and carriage with three female companions walking beside him. We looked at him and then agreed that everyone's pilgrimage is different.

Leaving the city of Sahagún, we walked through the Arco de San Benito to the alternate route that follows the old Roman road to our next stop. Ecstatic with the promise of a private room, we set off to the Calzadilla de los Hermanillos carrying extra water and food. There would be fewer towns for provisions along this ancient route.

We explored the village at sunset and passed a wall of climbing roses. "Mother's Day roses!" Patti exclaimed. Excitedly, we headed back to the *albergue* for a pilgrim's dinner, a private room, our own bath, and a glorious night's sleep free from the sounds of snoring pilgrims.

# Day 18

## Calzadilla de los Hermanillos to León
43.1 km/26.8 miles

Flocks of sheep roam large stretches of the Meseta, moving along ancient rights of way called "las cañadas".

Today's 27 miles started on the ancient Roman road, Calzada Romana. It is a quiet, desolate path with very little shade and no places to stop for food and water. We stocked up before we left. Eventually, the two paths converged and we arrived back on the *senda*. Once again, we were on the endless gravel path, and we would spend the rest of the day walking parallel or crisscrossing the busy highway with cars and huge trucks whizzing by heading to León...a disturbing intrusion from the modern world.

Midday, we stopped at a café, and as we walked out of the village, we found ourselves sharing the road with a herd of sheep. Delighted, we were swallowed up in a friendly sea of wool. We once again scanned the long stretch disappearing into the flat horizon. We could see pilgrims off in the distance and knew we were on the right path as we left the province of Palencia and crossed into the province of León.

EL CAMINO DE SANTIAGO
A SU PASO POR
PALENCIA

# Day 19

San Marcos

## A Day in León

Refreshed from a good night's sleep in a hotel, I wandered out to the plaza. Sitting on a bench, I stared at San Marcos for a long time while my sketch kit lay unopened next to me...

I sketch quickly with a pen and add loose, bright watercolor washes, capturing the moment, but this ancient building with its complex lines, angles, and details was going to take a slower, more studied line. I opened my sketchbook and started to draw. With this sketch, my art took on a deeper meaning—closer to understanding who I am and why I was here.

For most of the day, I mindfully and joyfully sketched the former monastery and hospital, which is now a restored Parador hotel, listening to the sounds of people enjoying the famous Plaza de San Marcos.

Leon Spain

"To be an artist is to believe in life"
—Henry Moore

# Day 20  León to Villar de Mazarife
## 22.2 km/13.8 miles

Leaving León, we crossed over the San Marcos Bridge following bronze scallop shell markers set into the pavement to the outskirts of the city. We took the longer alternate route away from the highway to the small town of Villar de Mazarife.

After checking into Tio Pepe's private *albergue*, Albergue Tio Pepe, we relaxed in the lively garden filled with pilgrims who were laughing and sharing stories. Drying laundry hung from everything imaginable.

I walked over to the village square with my sketch book and plastic bag of sketching tools. Sitting on a curb opposite the small village church and a statue of St James, I started to sketch with my two favorite pens and then splashed the sketch with watercolors. I immediately noticed how my brush goes right to the warm earthy colors of Spain. Just like all churches in the Meseta, there were storks perched in all the steeples, and I felt like I was being watched as I settled into the meditation of sketching.

Tomorrow we walk 20 miles to the town of Astorga...where they make chocolate—I can't wait!

Sculpture of St James the Great as a Camino pilgrim in front of the church.

Villar de Mazarife
Spain

## My favorite "go-to" pens

Carrying a minimal sketch kit, I needed
dependable pens that would give me
the varied lines for my sketches. The Staedtler
pigment liner pen 0.3 and the Kuretake brush
pen were invaluable tools on my creative
journey. (For a complete list of all my art
supplies, see page 89.)

*walking*

*and sketching*

STAEDLER pigment liner 0.3

# Day 21

## Villar de Mazarife to Astorga

31.2 km/19.4 miles

We awakened to a perfect day—clear and warm with blue sky and big puffy clouds. The ancient stone Cross of Santo Toribio, El Crucero de Santo Toribio, was at the highest point of our walk. This is where we stopped for a break. In the distance, we could see the old medieval Roman city built on top of a hill...Astorga.

A steep climb into the walled city was rewarded with charming architecture and lovely shops. Every other shop was devoted to **CHOCOLATE.** This city is serious about their chocolate!

Antoni Gaudí designed the Episcopal Palace of Astorga in the Catalan Modernisme style.

We checked in to our hotel and headed out to the famous Palacio Episcopal de Astorga. It was designed by the Spanish architect Antoni Gaudí and has his distinctive modern style. I sat and sketched until it was time to meet some pilgrim friends at an outdoor café on the Plaza Mayor. On our way back to the hotel, we sampled and bought plenty of delicious Astorga chocolate for the road. The following morning, we guiltlessly indulged in churros dipped in chocolate before our walk.

We left Astorga heading into the mountains toward the highest point of our route. We decided to stay in Foncebadón, a semi-abandoned village that was originally the home of a 12th century hermit who lived in this isolated mountain hamlet.

When we arrived, the *albergue* was packed with pilgrims looking for a place to sleep. We managed to squeeze our way to the check-in desk and claim our two reserved beds. The pilgrims at the end of the line slept on yoga mats in one of the out buildings near the goats.

That night we had the most delicious pilgrim's dinner of our entire walk. We all marveled at the flavorful vegetarian paella, fresh tossed salad made with vegetables from their garden, their homemade bread, and their fresh goat milk yogurt. Over bottles of wine, we told stories of who we were and shared Camino experiences.

We all laughed as Chris, a handsome young Brit, told of discovering one of the goats eating his favorite pair of underwear that was hanging out to dry on the shrubbery.

Later in the bunkroom, it was warm, and the air was thick, as we were packed in with beds pushed together to make room for more pilgrims. I finally made it through the line to the shared bath, slipped into my sleeping bag, and stared right into the face of the guy in the next bed...

Enjoying the setting full moon
as we walked out of Foncebadón
to La Cruz de Ferro.

# Day 23
## Foncebadón to Molinaseca
21 km/13 miles

La Cruz de Ferro is at the highest point of our journey. It is a pilgrim's tradition to place a rock at the base of this holy iron cross, which is said to be thousands of years old and to symbolize the "casting off of your sorrows." I carried two rocks that I found on the beach near my home, and Patti brought a heart shaped rock to honor this tradition. Up early, we placed our rocks at the cross while we watched the full moon set over the snow covered mountains. Then we made our way down a steep, rocky trail lined with purple lavender, as well as yellow and white Spanish broom in full bloom. We passed the abandoned village of Manjarín, a *refugio,* or shelter, now owned by Tomás, a modern Knight Templar, who makes the village a population of one.

La Cruz de Ferro
Spain

236.9 km/147.2 miles Santiago 57

# Day 24 Molinaseca to Villafranca del Bierzo
30.9 km/19.2 miles

It was a wild night of snoring in a roomful of pilgrims at the *albergue* in Molinaseca. After much tossing and turning, adjusting my earplugs, and using all my will to make it stop, I finally got up, located the culprit, and gently shook the bed. Then after several attempts of shaking the bed with all my might, I finally managed to get things quieted down. The rest of my roommates seemed to be dead to the world and sleeping soundly...how do they do it?

We got an early start to Villafranca del Bierzo. We watched the moon set over the mountains as we headed into the city of Ponferrada. We wended our way through the quiet streets and came upon the famous Castillo de los Templarios. We found a quaint sidewalk café and enjoyed a *caf*é *con leche* and a tortilla while we stared up at this ominous 12th century Templar castle. I did a quick sketch to finish later before we headed out.

We were now ready to face the next 15 miles through small villages, farmlands, foothills, and vineyards before reaching Villafranca del Bierzo.

Castillo de los Templarios, a 12th century castle of the Knights Templar.

*Iglesias San Francisco  Villafranca Spain*

As we reached the outskirts of Villafranca del Bierzo, we saw a taxi stop in front of an *albergue*. Out poured Wim, Erwin, and Lawrence. We laughed, waved, and went in search of our hotel. We had come to understand the phrase... "The Camino provides."

216.2 km/134.3 miles *Santiago*

# Day 25 Villafranca del Bierzo to Laguna de Castilla
27.6 km/17.1 miles

Albergue Escrela Laguna de Castilla

On Day 25, I walked alone because Patti was down with a stomach virus. While looking quite peaked, she checked the guidebook and suggested I take the alternate route, which was away from the busy highway. I found my way to the start of a very demanding 17-mile uphill trail along a ridge with spectacular views of the Carpathian Mountains in Galicia. I was very aware of being alone and seeming to be the only pilgrim who chose this arduous route. There were no arrows or shell markers. However, the occasional wad of toilet paper assured me that pilgrims had walked this path. I finally decided to find my way down to the valley floor where I happily joined Lawrence, Wim, and Erwin, who were taking a break at a café in a tiny hamlet along the river. I was thankful for a break and a Coca-Cola Zero before continuing our ascent.

That night we stayed at an *albergue* high in the mountains where the cows, chickens, and the local *albergue* dog shared the plaza with us pilgrims. Patti, who was still recovering, went to bed early while I sketched, did laundry, and swapped Camino stories as the sun set over the mountains.

# Day 26  Laguna de Castilla to Triacastela
23.8 km/14.8 miles

The centuries old circular stone mountain dwellings of O Cebreiro called pallozas.

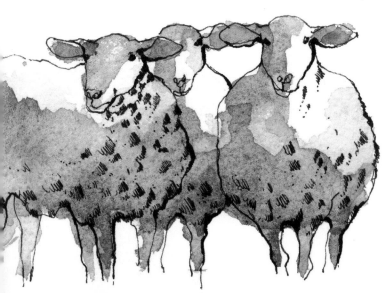

We began our day with a steep walk into the mountains, crossing into the rainy province of Galicia. The now muddy Camino path cut through miles of rolling green hills dotted with grazing sheep. We could hear the sound of cowbells, a sound not heard since the Pyrenees, which seemed like ages ago. We wandered through the ancient medieval village of O Cebriero with its centuries old unique mountain dwellings called pallozas.

Our drizzly walk downhill took us along rock-walled paths, through wooded areas, tiny hamlets, and local farmyards. Passing through a small cluster of old moss covered stone buildings, a very old woman stepped out holding a steaming plate of crepes, hoping to entice hungry pilgrims for a euro—"No, *muchas gracias,*" we said, smiled, and hurried on.

Upon arriving in Triacastela, we saw two burros in the field munching on the tall, green grass while their owners cared for them and settled them in for the night. I sketched while listening to them describe their journey on the Camino with burros. As she stroked and spoke softly to Lulu, she explained that each burro was carrying a pilgrim's pack, along with a burro feed bucket and other things a burro would need for a long journey. According to the pilgrim, burros are very loyal and extremely social animals and should never live or travel alone...so *dos burros*.

"Berce do Camiño" · Triacastela · Lugo · Albergue

Triacastela
Spain

# Dogs are...

## much like the Camino—
both have lessons if you are listening.

We met some wonderful dogs... and cats along the way. Each one I sketched or photographed reminded me of how much I missed my dog, Sophie, waiting for me back home. There was the amazing Jean Luc who guided us over the Pyrenees; a formally dressed cat who was staring down some rodent hole in the vineyards of La Rioja; Pip, a Corgi from Australia, who was wearing a cool "Camino bandana," and  I bought one just like it; a scruffy little dog with the most amazing under bite as we waited to check in to an *albergue* in Molinaseca; a German shepherd in almost every town; and the two sweet dogs walking from St Jean to Santiago with their owner Christian from Romania.

# Day 27  Triacastela to Sarria
### 23.4 km/14.5 miles

The final third of the Camino runs through the province of Galicia. It is much colder, wetter, and greener. We walked by miles of stonewalls dividing brilliant green pastures. The patchwork landscape reminded us of Ireland. We passed several high stone crosses honoring The Way and the pilgrims who made the journey to Santiago over the centuries.

We arrived in Sarria cold and wet from our wind and rain soaked walk. We climbed steep steps, wending our way through the streets of this lively Celtic city in search of our *albergue*. After checking in, we organized our packs and sleeping quarters and hung our wet clothes out to dry. We headed out to explore Sarria and find a pulperia for the regional favorite *Pulpo a la Gallega*—grilled octopus Galicia style. *¡Delicioso!*

After a meal and drinks with some of our favorite pilgrim friends, I set out to buy ponchos...weather forecast for the next week...**Rain...Rain...Rain...**

In front of a crackling fire back at the *albergue,* we shared Camino stories with other pilgrims while I sketched several of them and then took a photo of them holding their portraits. We handed out the portraits as gifts as the clock struck 10:00 and *albergue* rules kicked in...**lights out!**

# Day 28 Sarria to Portomarín
22.4 km / 13.9 miles

It's raining in Galicia so everyone, including the burros, is wearing some kind of waterproof covering to keep dry. Last night, I scored the last two ponchos at an outdoor clothing store. One was bright yellow and the other was a dull green. I had a feeling I was going to be wearing the yellow one. While I was walking out of Sarria that morning, a fellow pilgrim pointed, laughed, and remarked that I look strangely like Big Bird...

It rained all day. The wind was fierce. We arrived in Portomarín cold, wet, and thankful for our ponchos. In the cozy warmth of a café, I sketched and Patti wrote in her journal. I noticed a hair salon across the street and I abruptly left to get my bangs trimmed. When I arrived back at the *taberna*, Patti said I had an odd shape to my bangs. She told me not to worry because she could fix it. Back at the *albergue*, she evened up my bangs with a dull pair of office scissors while other pilgrims gave us some advice as my bangs got shorter and shorter.

# Day 29 Portomarín to Palas de Rei
24.8 km/15.4 miles

Late that afternoon, I sketched in the café at Albergue Buen Camino, where the walls were filled with eclectic pilgrim paraphernalia and coins from all over the world. Later, we ventured out in search of a *supermercado* to buy ingredients to cook a simple dinner in the kitchen at the *albergue*. Patti, being tall, deftly wove her way around the kitchen, taking turns with burners and sharing pots and pans with other shorter pilgrims who were cooking French and Korean meals. The smells were amazing, and in the end... voilà, as pilgrim Michele announced, everyone's meals were ready. We sat at tables enjoying our own regional comfort food. Michele and Francoise offered us some of their crusty Galician bread to go with our American fare, and with much gratitude, we were able to enjoy its hearty, chewy goodness.

That night, as I lay snuggled in my sleeping bag, I marveled as I counted five languages being quietly spoken from all the beds in the room. Just another night on the Camino...
**let the snoring begin....**

The stone walls of Albergue Buen Camino are filled with years of pilgrim memorabilia.

# Day 30 Palas de Rei to Ribadiso
25.8 km/16 miles

We experienced another misty day in Galicia while passing through beautiful oak woodlands, fragrant eucalyptus forests, and traditional Galician villages. The path was narrow and muddy and we were thankful for our hiking poles as we crossed several shallow rivers while carefully hopping from stone to stone. Not only did we share the path with many pilgrims, but several times farmers with herds of cows would come clumping around a bend. Warned by the sound of their cowbells, we would step aside and let these huge beautiful beasts pass. I remember thinking that I would probably leave my shoes in Spain...

We ended the day by crossing over a beautiful ancient 6th century bridge that spans the Río Iso and into the tiny hamlet of Ribadiso. We found our *albergue*, scored lower bunks, and went off to enjoy a festive dinner with a group of pilgrim friends.

ALBERGUE
Los Caminantes
Tlno.: 647 020 600
RIBADISO - Arzúa - A Coruña

# Day 31 Ribadiso to Arca O Pino
22.1 km/13.7 miles

Our walk would be a lot like yesterday's walk. We ambled on natural pathways through shaded woodlands with calla lilies and the strong scent of eucalyptus. While walking through Galicia, we saw small wooden sheds perched on stone bases. We discovered that they are *horreos*, long narrow granaries used to hold and ripen all forms of grain, corn, and farm produce.

The horreo is a typical Galician granary that's raised above ground to avoid rodents.

Pimentos de Padron

Todo para el
Peregrino

ARCA - O PINO

Arca-O Pino, Spain

After a little exploring and a late afternoon drink at an outdoor café, I was dragged into a lively sports bar. As we enjoyed our favorite tapas—Pimentos de Padrón—Patti, a lifelong sports fan, was in her element. She kept an eye on the Stanley Cup playoffs, but she wasn't quite sure which Madrid soccer team to root for during World Cup play. The whole thing was terribly confusing to me, so I just sketched.

On the last day, I was the first one to leave a room filled with twenty sleeping pilgrims from all over the world. I tried not to make too much noise as I slipped my plastic bag of cosmetics out of my pack and tiptoed into the large shared bathroom. I looked in the mirror and there I was, as usual, with my hair sticking out all over the place and dark circles under my eyes. I brushed my teeth, put my hair up, and added bright red lipstick.

Suddenly the *albergue* came to life as pilgrims laced up their boots, grabbed their packs, and headed out the door wishing each other a final *¡Buen Camino!*

Ready to go, I hoisted my pack on my back for the last time as we fell into step with other pilgrims who followed the yellow arrows out of town and through the last of the shaded sweet smelling eucalyptus forest. As we got closer to the city, we walked on asphalt streets, and it became more crowded as more pilgrims joined the one-day route into Santiago.

We were quiet as we walked, lost in our thoughts and reflections of thirty-two days on the Camino. We passed the monument at Monte do Gozo, the Hill of Joy, where we got our first glimpse of the Santiago de Compostela Cathedral.

Following the sound of bagpipes, we walked through narrow cobblestone streets, under a stone arch, and onto the Praza do Obradoiro. As we stood in front of the Santiago de Compostela Cathedral, we felt utter elation for completing what we had set out to do. Overwhelmed with emotion, I became aware of a hint of sadness that the journey was over...or had it just begun?...

So, with our pilgrim's passport in hand, we went with the rest of the arriving pilgrims to get our official document of completion... the *compostela*.

# Grateful

## We step into the Cathedral in awe of what is before us.

The famous Botafumeiro is a huge incense burner filled with frankincense used in ancient times for arriving tired and unwashed pilgrims. It was believed that incense smoke could help clean the air in the time of plagues and epidemics. The tradition continues today. At the end of the pilgrim's mass, an enormous pendulum swings through the center of the cathedral, leaving behind a trail of smoke and strong fragrance.

At the end of the long center aisle is a blazing gold altar with the statue of St James. Here, in his gilded splendor, was the mystical man we had been hearing and talking about for thirty-two days and 500 miles.

We climbed the stairs that lead to an area behind the altar, where we were told we could touch and embrace this amazing statue. We stood in a long slow-moving line walking up a tiny narrow staircase. Overwhelmed, I wrapped my arms around St. James and gave him a big hug. Later, over a glass of champagne, I confessed to having gone back several times for a few more hugs.

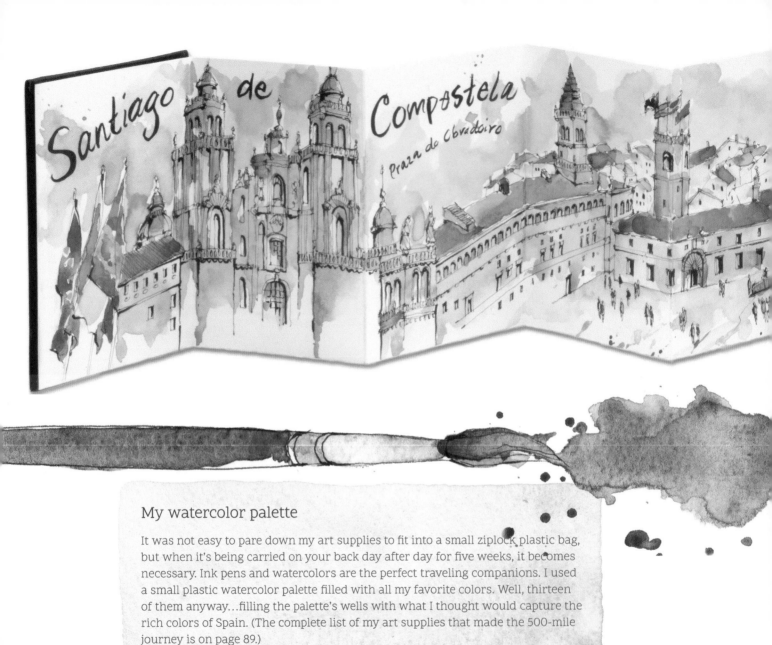

## My watercolor palette

It was not easy to pare down my art supplies to fit into a small ziplock plastic bag, but when it's being carried on your back day after day for five weeks, it becomes necessary. Ink pens and watercolors are the perfect traveling companions. I used a small plastic watercolor palette filled with all my favorite colors. Well, thirteen of them anyway...filling the palette's wells with what I thought would capture the rich colors of Spain. (The complete list of my art supplies that made the 500-mile journey is on page 89.)

New Gamboge

Quinacridone Gold

Cadmium Red Medium

Opera Pink

Alizarin Crimson

Green Gold/ Sap Green

# The Camino is very much like sketching, the joy is found not by finishing, but in the act of doing.

The day was cold and drizzly, but I managed to find a place to sketch the Santiago de Compostela Cathedral and the Praza do Obradoiro. I found several tall windows in an ornate ballroom on the third floor of the Hotel Parador de Santiago de Compostela. Using a 6" x 40" accordion sketchbook, I captured the panoramic view that lay before me.

As I settled into my first window seat, I thought, *It took almost 150 years to build this cathedral, so I could probably take a mere 150 minutes to draw it.*

I ended up spending the afternoon going from window to window. I was caught up in the pure joy of sketching and realizing that this is who I am. It was one of those blissful "moments of being".

Cerulean Blue

Ultramarine Blue

Yellow Ochre

Burnt Sienna

Burnt Umber

Shadow Violet

# Stamping Our Way to Santiago
Colorful Camino stamps serve as proof of our 500-mile walk.

Credencial de Peregrino—
Pilgrim's Passport

**Patti:** I take pleasure in discovering things for myself. To wonder, to question, and to conclude on my own. So, it is in that spirit that I set out on the Camino. I had no preconceived notion about what the journey would provide or teach, but I was open to learning and was curious and reflective as it unfolded. The Camino did not disappoint. It pushed my introverted limits, allowed me to see the human side of all types of people, and gave me the opportunity to discover that I could grow a bit more as a person. For that, I will always be grateful.

**Jennifer:** I often think of my time on the Camino. The "simple" life of waking early, walking with the rising sun, and listening to bird songs. Walking through vineyards, fields of wheat, rye, oats, and alongside snow-covered mountains with foothills of purple lavender. My morning *café con leche*, an afternoon exploring a new town, catching up with fellow pilgrims, and finding a place to sketch at the end of each amazing day.

It has taken me awhile to understand the significance of my pilgrimage on the Camino. This 500-mile journey taught me to believe in my real artist self—I make art, therefore I am.

# Camino Must-Haves

**Your pilgrimage begins** the day you make the decision to go. We researched backpacks and how much weight to carry, whether to wear boots or trail runners, what clothes to wear, and how many of each item—pants, shirts, jackets, socks, and underwear, cosmetics, toiletries, first aid kit, and electronics. The list is long and takes careful consideration because of the weight on your back. Once you are out there...stuff happens...rain, rain, and more rain, wet clothes, laundry, blisters, heat, thirst, sleepless nights, community bunkrooms, washrooms, and sharing...lots and lots of sharing...

### A Pilgrim's Guide to the Camino de Santiago by John Brierley

This indispensable guidebook helps you navigate your way across the Camino. It's filled with essential information on the daily walks, what to expect and plan for, what to see, and most importantly, where to stay.

### First Aid Kit

Your feet take a beating on the Camino, and here are a few must-haves. Anti-blister balm: This balm reduces friction that could result in blisters. We slathered it on our feet before putting on socks and shoes. Another must have is silicone gel toe caps that protected and healed the few blisters we acquired from day after day on the trail.

### Comfortable Shoes

These will be on your feet most of the day so comfort and fit are key. I would recommend a lightweight trail running shoe.

### Hiking Poles

Simple lightweight poles are a must. They will improve your balance on uneven surfaces, especially when wearing a pack. They also reduce wear and tear on your ankles, knees, and hips and improve the efficiency of each step.

## A Good Pack

Make sure you get the right size, the right fit, and the right weight. My pack was a bit too heavy and my shoulders screamed with pain by Day 3. I ended up improvising along the way—taking breaks and Ibuprofen. Whining a bit also seemed to help. I finally managed to cobble together a makeshift padding solution using large sponges slipped inside sock liners and attached to the underside of my straps. Once again, "The Camino provides," but get a good pack that fits you. You will be happy you did.

## Rain Gear

A decent raincoat is a necessity. It also keeps you warm and protects you from the wind. Because of the amount of rain, we ended up buying ponchos to cover ourselves and our packs. It would be better to find room in your pack for a lightweight poncho...especially when you are in Galicia.

See a complete list of what was in my pack on the next four pages.

## What I Wore

GORE-TEX® Rainjacket

Soft Shell Jacket (2)

T-Shirts (3)

Dress

Lightweight Wind Pants

Capri Lycra Hiking Pants (2)

PJ's/Long Underwear

Bras (2)

Underwear (3)

Flats • Flip-Flops

## My Gear

Hiking Poles
Sunglasses
Fanny Pack
Sleeping Bag
Hiking Boots
Socks (2) Pair
Travel Towel
Headlamp
Cell Phone
eReader
Poncho

# Body & Health

- Hair Brush
- Hair Scrunchie
- Electric Toothbrush
- Toothpaste
- 3-in-1 Soap
  (Shampoo, Body Wash, Laundry Soap)
- Face Cream—SPF 30
- Ibuprophen
- Bandages
- Moleskin
- Gel Toe Caps
- Anti Blister Balm
- Ear Plugs
- Lip Balm
- Coconut Body Mist
- Concealor
- Bright Red Lipstick

hair scrunchie

ear plugs

CHAPSTICK

3 in 1
Shampoo
Body
Wash
Laundry
Soap

TOOTHPASTE

FACE
cream

SPF
30

Ibuprophe

Russian RED

Concealor

ANTi
Blister
Balm

gel
toe caps

coconut
BODY
MIST

## My Sketch Kit

Staedtler Pen 0.3, 0.1

Kuretake Brush Pen

Mechanical Pencil

Kneaded Eraser

Plastic Palette
(My favorite tube colors added)

Da Vinci Travel Brush

Niji Waterbrush

Collapsible Cup

Clips

Spray Water Bottle

8 x 5.5 Moleskine
Watercolor Sketchbooks (2)
(Covers taken off to lighten weight)

4 x 6 Sennelier Accordian
Sketchbook

Staedtler Pigment liner 0.3

Kuretake brush pen

mechanical pencil

da Vinci 10

kneaded eraser

Water

Spray Bottle

# About the Authors

**Jennifer Lawson**—Author, Illustrator

Finding her way into commercial art after college, Jennifer spent twenty years as vice president of creative design for LL Bean in Freeport, Maine. In her post-corporate career, she has worked for more than ten years as a freelance creative director, designer, and illustrator. In between freelance jobs, Jennifer picked up a pen and started to draw. It changed her life and how she sees the world.

She has sketched and painted her way up and down the Maine coast and throughout the United States. She has sketched through Paris, Barcelona, Lisbon, over the Inca Trail to the ruins of Machu Picchu, while living on the island of Bali, Indonesia, climbing to the top of Mt Kilimanjaro, and most recently while walking on the Camino de Santiago pilgrimage across Spain.

Through her 500-mile journey as a "walker/sketcher/pilgrim", she discovered her true artist's self. Jennifer is rarely seen without a pen and sketchbook. She finds the inspiration to draw from even the simplest of surroundings.

**Patricia Lennon**—Contributor, Marketer

Patricia is not one to sit still for long. She enjoys seeking the next interesting idea. Because of a passion for fashion and retail, Patricia found herself traveling worldwide during an over twenty-five year career as an innovator in product development, marketing, and sales. By creating her own consulting firm, she has managed to find the balance and freedom to explore the world.

Walking the Camino de Santiago gave Patricia the time to fine-tune the essence of being present, gain a fresh perspective, and apply the lessons she learned about the human condition to her own life. She takes great pleasure in doing all the things she once put off until "someday".

21945656R00054

Printed in Poland
by Amazon Fulfillment
Poland Sp. z o.o., Wrocław